Bouldering

LEVEL 8

/y/ou/

DECODABLES BY jump!

Teaching Tips

Purple Level 8

This book focuses on the phonemes **/y/ou/**.

Before Reading

- Discuss the title. Ask readers what they think the book will be about. Have them support their answer.
- Discuss the book's focused phonemes. Explain that /y/ can have four different sounds: /y/, long /e/, long /i/, and short /i/. Explain that /ou/ can have two different sounds: /ow/ or /oo/. Give examples of each.

Read the Book

- Encourage readers to read independently, either aloud or silently to themselves.
- Prompt readers to break down unfamiliar words into units of sound and string the sounds together to form the words. Then, ask them to look for context clues to see if they can figure out what these words mean. Discuss new vocabulary to confirm meaning.
- Urge readers to point out when each focused phonics phoneme appears in the text. What sound does it make?

After Reading

- Ask readers comprehension questions about the book. What is a group of holds called?
- Encourage readers to think of other words with the /y/ or /ou/ phoneme. On a separate sheet of paper, have them write the words into columns by sound.

5357 Penn Avenue South
Minneapolis, MN 55419
www.jumplibrary.com

Decodables by Jump! are published by Jump! Library.

Library of Congress Cataloging-in-Publication Data is available at www.loc.gov or upon request from the publisher.

ISBN: 979-8-88996-891-7 (hardcover)
ISBN: 979-8-88996-892-4 (paperback)
ISBN: 979-8-88996-893-1 (ebook)

Photo Credits

Images are courtesy of Shutterstock.com. With thanks to Getty Images, Thinkstock Photo and iStockphoto. Cover – Aleksandar Jankovic. p4–5 – zhukovvvlad, nuclear_lily. p6–7 – Duet PandG, Jacob Lund. p8–9 – frantic00, Brian Maag. p10–11 – UfaBizPhoto, Zakirov Aleksey. p12–13 – michelangeloop, UfaBizPhoto. p14–15 – asife, Andrew Angelov. p16 – Shutterstock.

Which of these words have the same **ou** sound as **house**?

mouse

could

sprout

shout

group

soup

bounce

Have you ever been bouldering? Bouldering is a sport that is all about finding the best way to climb to the top of a rock by choosing the best holds.

If you go bouldering at a gym, there will not be real rock. Bouldering gyms have lots of panels covered in different-shaped holds.

A group of holds is called a problem. Before boulderers try to get to the top of a problem, they get a good look at it from the ground to scout out the best route to take.

Boulderers may have to try the same problem over and over to find the best way up.

In bouldering gyms, problems are set by people called route setters. They drill different kinds of holds onto the panels. A big, round hold is called a sloper.

A small hold is called a crimp. Boulderers need strong fingers to grip little holds like crimps. A crimp only has space for the very tips of the fingers.

Without the right gear, it would be easy to slip. Boulderers carry a pouch of powder with them to keep their fingers dry.

Boulderers use tight, rubber footwear too. Rubber is sticky and gives the boulderer's feet good grip, even on tiny footholds. They can also hook their heels onto holds and trust that they will not slip.

Bouldering routes are normally pretty close to the ground, so boulderers do not have to worry too much about getting hurt if they do slip. There are soft mats under the problems too.

Even with soft mats, boulderers could still get hurt if they land badly. Boulderers may have people called spotters around them to help them drop safely onto the mats.

Bouldering is most fun when you go as a group. Gyms have easy problems for new boulderers and hard problems for expert boulderers.

If you go on a bouldering trip outside, make sure that you bring safety mats. Some routes may not be safe even with mats, so never try to boulder without an expert there to help.

Say the name of each object below. Is the "ou" in each an /ow/ sound or an /oo/ sound?

1...2...3

count

toucan

mouse

you